WOLVES

Sandie Lee Books

Wolves

Wolves are related to dogs. They were the first animal to ever be domesticated (or tamed) by man. This happened over 10,000 years ago. There are around 70 different types of wolves in the world. Wolves have appeared as villains in stories and in myths. Some cultures place high value on the wolf for its qualities. In this article we are going to discover many more cool facts about wolves. So let's get started.

Where in the World?

Did you know wolves can be found all over the world? Wolves have a larger territory than any other animal on the planet. They can be found In North America, Europe and Asia. The wolf will live in forested regions, mountains, plains and even swampy areas. They are highly adaptable!

The Body of a Wolf

Did you know wolves can grow to be around 175 pounds? Wolves have thick coats that protect them from the cold air. Their muzzles are long and they have a broad head with pointy ears that stand straight up. Their eyes are slanted and their tails are long and bushy.

What a Wolf Eats

Did you know wolves are carnivorous? Wolves like to eat meat. The wolf hunts caribou, bison, moose, deer and other mammals big and small. Sometimes if a pack of wolves are starving they will kill and eat the weakest member of the pack. Wolves have also been known to kill domesticated cats and dogs.

The Wolf's Special Ability

Did you know the sense of smell is the wolf's strongest sense? The wolf's nose looks a lot like any dog's nose, but it is highly tuned. The nose of a wolf can smell 12 times better than a dog and 100 times better than we humans. The wolf uses this sense to locate prey and to avoid predators.

The Wolf as a Predator

Did you know wolves hunt as a pack? A pack of wolves will use their powerful noses to track their prey. They always stay upwind, so the prey cannot detect them. Wolves will look for the weakest member of a herd to catch and kill. The wolf takes down its prey from around the neck.

The Wolf as Prey

Did you know that the wolf have no natural enemies except for man? Man has hunted the wolf for its fur and for its tail. Sometimes farmers will kill wolves if they are being a nuisance around their land. This is done to protect the cattle and other farm animals.

Wolf Talk

Did you know that wolves can communicate? Probably the most common sound we hear a wolf make is its howl. Along with the eerie howl, wolves will also yip, whine and growl. Wolves will communicate with each other in the pack. Plus, mom with her pups will make gentle sounds to reassure them.

Mom and Babies

Did you know the mother wolf can give birth to anywhere between 4 to 7 pups? The mother wolf will find a den to have her cubs in. This can be a cave, a hollow log or a burrow along a sand bank. The pups are born blind, deaf and helpless.

Wolves at Rest

Did you know wolves sleep most of the day? Wolves are nocturnal animals. This means they sleep most of the day and are active at night. When the wolves rest, they will find a shady place in the summer and a warm place in the winter. They will all sleep together to stay warm.

Wolves at Play

Did you know wolves like to play? Wolves play much like domesticated dogs do. They will run and chase after each other. They will also play with sticks or branches and practice hunting skills as pups. Wolf pups learn much from playing with each other and by watching the adult wolves.

Life of a Wolf

Did you know wolves are very family orientated? Most wolves live in packs that consist of family members. One male and one female will be the leaders. They are called the "alpha." The weakest wolf will be the last one to eat and is only given the leftovers from a kill. Wolves can live to be around 18 years-old.

The Gray Wolf

The gray wolf is the largest of all the wolves. It is found in remote areas of North Africa, North America and Eurasia. This species looks like a German shepherd or malamute dog. The numbers of this wolf have dropped from 2 million to around 200,000. You can see and hear these wolves in Yellowstone National Park.

The Arabian Wolf

The arabian wolf is the smallest of all the wolf species. It only weighs about 40 pounds. It has short greyish-beige fur and very large ears. Their eyes are yellow with black pupils. This wolf is found in Arabia. Because of the shortage of food, this species only packs during mating season.

The Arctic Wolf

The Arctic wolf lives in Northern Europe, Northern Canada, Alaska and parts of Greenland and Iceland. Its fur is white in color and very thick. This keeps it warm in the sub-zero temperatures. It is medium-size, weighing around 80 pounds. Because of where it lives, the Arctic wolf spends 5 months of the year in total darkness.

Quiz

Question 1: What common animal is the wolf related to?

Answer 1: The dog

Question 2: Where do wolves live?

Answer 2: Mountains, forests, plains and swampy regions

Question 3: How many pups can a mother wolf have?

Answer 3: She can have from 4 to 7 pups

Question 4: What are the leaders of a wolf pack called?

Answer 4: Alphas

Question 5: Which wolf lives in the cold regions of the world?

Answer 5: The Arctic wolf

Thank you for checking out another addition from Sandie Lee Books! Make sure to check out Amazon.com for many other great titles.

www.ingramcontent.com/pod-product-compliance
Lightning Source LLC
Chambersburg PA
CBHW050803290526
45792CB00008B/2302